THE RECKONING OF JEANNE D'ANTIETAM

THE TEST SITE POETRY SERIES

Claudia Keelan, University of Nevada, Las Vegas, *Series Editor*

The Test Site Poetry Series is a collaboration between the University of Nevada, Las Vegas's Black Mountain Institute, *Witness* and *The Believer*, and the University of Nevada Press. Each year, the series editor along with an advisory board, which includes Sherwin Bitsui, Donald Revell, Sasha Steensen, and Ronaldo Wilson, will select a winner and a runner-up. The selected winners will be published by the University of Nevada Press as part of this series.

Winning books engage the perilous conditions of life in the twenty-first century, as they pertain to issues of social justice and the earth. They demonstrate an ethos that considers the human condition in inclusive love and sympathy, while offering the same in consideration with the earth.

Refugia by Kyce Bello

Riddle Field by Derek Thomas Dew

Mouth of the Earth by Sarah P. Strong

A Sybil Society by Katherine Factor

Interior Femme by Stephanie Berger

Joyful Orphan by Mark Irwin

The Reckoning of Jeanne d'Antietam by Matthew Moore

The Reckoning of
Jeanne d'Antietam

POEMS

Matthew Moore

UNIVERSITY OF NEVADA PRESS | *Reno & Las Vegas*

University of Nevada Press | Reno, Nevada 89557 USA
www.unpress.nevada.edu
Copyright © 2023 by Matthew Moore
All rights reserved

Manufactured in the United States of America

FIRST PRINTING

Cover illustration: *Bombardment and capture of Fort Hindman, Arkansas Post, Ark. Jany. 11th 1863,* Currier and Ives. Courtesy of the Library of Congress.

LIBRARY OF CONGRESS CATALOGING-IN-PUBLICATION DATA
Names: Moore, Matthew (Poet), author.
Title: The reckoning of Jeanne d'Antietam : poems / Matthew Moore.
Other titles: Test site poetry series.
Description: Reno ; Las Vegas : University of Nevada Press, [2022] |
Series: Test site poetry series |
Summary: "*The Reckoning of Jeanne d'Antietam* is a book of history poems that circle the U.S. Civil War. *The Reckoning of Jeanne d'Antietam* is unlike any poetry collection that readers have encountered before. Moore makes incursions into the histories and beliefs which his poems circle primarily through architectures of sound, but also via ancillary histories, histories stacked upon histories, densely and visibly scrawled."—Provided by publisher.
Identifiers: LCCN 2022030935 | ISBN 9781647790820 (paperback) | ISBN 9781647790837 (ebook)
Subjects: LCSH: United States—History—Civil War, 1861–1865—Poetry. | LCGFT: Poetry.
Classification: LCC PS3613.O56527 R43 2022 | DDC 811/.6—dc23/eng/20220715
LC record available at https://lccn.loc.gov/2022030935

It is true I wished to escape; and so I wish still;
is not this lawful for all prisoners.

—JEANNE D'ARC

Contents

THE RECKONING OF JEANNE D'ANTIETAM

The Sound Earth

Incursion is the speech sound measures and

Stands against, speech act blurred to substance, but what for, unless to circle
*   forward facing back*
Toward Reconstruction, toward the unhealed sound, needled in the patterns
*   in the activity of this*
Colony, playing out permanent contours to materials and color, charged
*   with: who is here, who is*

at-large, in my exterminating action, syntax—

I could answer: the reckoning of Jeanne d'Antietam, to hold out
*   purposefully, even dogmatically,*
To sound against theme, narrative, through-line, whatever cannot wait for
*   syntax that's this early,*
To put history in its own spanner, you send down for the reckoning of
*   Jeanne d'Antietam, history*

the present surface-tension I refrain against—

Onlooking in each word is action's negation, some sea fort Sumter, that
*   destruction, inculpation, civilization. I, myself, want to dig into the fort,*
*   what I oppose to sound, opposed, sung onto as structure because time*
*   unburies and buries speech, sand, the first obstruction to goodness by the*

sea, a hut for holding out in occupied terroir.

On dry land the sounds of the modern hear unison as none listen. Union is
*   over. Circus maximus, reconstructed as fence-the-world, I refrain, from*
*   you, from commentary poetries and histories,*
From death by water, I refrain, toward you, toward gorgons, toward words,
*   tho in terror and time*

More awful, more awful than that, that names can know and cannot
   know, is this, the needle, the
Toy humanism, sentiment, whiteness, the camel, the eye—: whatever
   imparts a Puritan desire to
Diminish scale, unlikeness, disproportion, that this, about you, moves you,
   about the correctional

   facilities, faculties, fecundities and felicities,

Which present tension holds out measured against, the sound earth makes
   inaudible to live—that

   survives without likeness. Is that heard here.

Leviathan

Any sprig that touches
Air touches water—
A blow in the heart blows the wall—
After debt is a circle
Arrived around valleys licked
A thread greener than
A matter of time—now shearing season—
Astronomers prod
Angles parallel to the ram—
Against sacrifice
Agamemnon makes waste
Achilles bloodies
Angles parallel to remains—
Apiaries muck out stables
Awash in honey or shit luck
As in uncanny valleys
Air touches wetnesses—
A horizon grows train horns
Around yourself the road—
Apex counterflow
Addled what mystery is
Aftermath the sea slurred clear—
After this hour another I come—
An ass braying on
Any sprig that touches

I

Needle

Sills rows plot winch, a grief
Opens on open disproportion, against
Seatide clouds longed longed
Shut. On a retch walk, I dog the chop
Before I am after American gleans, at
Nadir—Reconstructions shed
Honor cavillations raise and sanitize any
Quod I pitchpole under spray you envoy.

Undo the day, defile its fetid
Route, arrow penetralia nock, a string
Subconscious, conscience is
A tender thought racks loose on cross-
Hairs burnt into a spleen, comb-stung
Hairs teeth touch, nearer than
Thunder, set down inside barrels, bigger
Even, when rolled down a sky with stair.

Need will be somebody's wet
Vertigo, promise and stranger, rankle
Transit, one way out of here, through
Blush tirade, a kiss, enclaved,
Blanched at both ends, by fog, or pus.

Listen, now, climb the ever-turned beam
Down its listless rope. Sky fines. Sunshine
Fines. A white band of black glister. Crassest
Decanted, praise and debt measure
Before scales snake the compass's bar.

Speculative Fire

Nonpareil retablo, paramour, troth clouts
Into sex force that wheels lays
Draws a bead on dew point for the calyx,
And, at the clout, at sex, cusps
Clouts charm: trust. Janey in a wax you
Stand on your head, un-gloved
In a tally. Empty every bath rings a fault
Grace fruits, stand-
Ards on rain, drowned conies,
Vair azimuths on
A meridian, nothing is
Civil in the shaft space downcast.

A fracked glass mirrors in the dock, slides
A bilge over Janey in her retrial,
Here comes every swimmer a swim exiles.
Janey floats, sags, a wax mouth
Tastes tasteless, obverse each breach rides.
Joan of Arc sounds rotten lobed
A leaf, a street in sacks, shore soldiers pile.
Occupy, Janey, the
Juniper hours on a clothes nail,
Its affection of
Conservative recourse
Pretends the Republic is natural,

Of Nature, Danton worried, Robespierre
Suffered. Old life study wound.
Mourners index dew, you sit at guttation
Starved for sobs at a lay sound.

Old stories stepped on by inefficacies joy
Shudders, a valley in red shoes,
Not and nothing but seen through thought.
Set I my tongue to
Her pace, unprintable wounds
Protract to you,
She has—She bids me,
Shield my privation without pity.

Antiphon: For the Solar Rooster of St. John

I. Rose Mallow

No life not to mourn. Dithyramb then till.
Cries oar the stone tide, harrow
Parageneses laughing gulls face and mill
The white cliffs, losses, barrow.
The white horizon is lime as rind preens
The cloacal kiss of ships keens
After knots rake rooster tails abaft holds.
Wind keeps, in sails, and holds.
    Death by water, St. John is the Immerser,
    The rooster's time's messenger,
    Salome is the sunray and cloudline pang.
    Sickle feather, cane wave, tang.
   Viridian cognomen bar by the pale quarry,
   O'er the sands, bears the shores,
   Populace schloss, O hell, the human aerie.
   Glossal crosses, saltire, the oars.
Sails, quartered, tarred, pinned, shit to chute,
Bored, holed, breaths, manifests,
Wings pierced through cane, poppy and onyx.
Hole in the head, base halo, lute.
    No death not to grieve. A forecastle mars.
    Cries ore the stone tide, Diderot
    Polished as reflects his passage an hour's
    Subtle plantation: light; shadow.
   Keeps, bolling seaside charnel, broke oar.
   Crow's row, rose mallow, o'er
   Paraph mist, wattle light the breakers ore,
   The white cliffs, losses, order.

II. Pon the Illegible Warrant

                  Sugar is the boiled surface, drowning
Chattel for taste in airless wells, and
                  Ardor landscapes of Poussin's kidney;
Ports bagasse foams, bled fuel pond,
                  Hybrid winds pinnated blades wind, blond;
Tower cultivars, Black Code fronds
                  Siren pon the double-consentless inner ear;
Petroglyphs, the littoral depressions
Property bags, at waste's gate, entropic dispossession in visible light's
      opaque blancmange,
                  O'er the living spoils, St. Cheesecloth's feast day,
      the wanting
Food, urn of love's ague, iron choux.
                  I shall paint my face with starvation fruit,
      Promontory, coast the shade
                  Of canebrake, round and round the cane,
      Nail paints Color Club sails
                  Reef solvents, to Carib airports, in vials:
"Sweet as Sugarcane." Ho!
                  Sugar is in love songs, enough, to finish
Atlas Novus, to light every
                  Iron stem, glass pane in *Arcades Project*,
To anchor, down to the last,
                  The black plates of the *Mnemosyne Atlas*.
By heat, the Sphinx ashens.
                  Night mordant whitens the bloody shirts lime
Factories debride, breed, security
                  Parchment sat pon the illegible warrant, rime
Of blood, air, the nacre of the sea.

III. *Two Needle Drops from the Annaberg Plantation Record*

".. and the word of God I prayed, and sought. I kidnapped and killed,
" tons, and the mystery of the cross, God's love, secured me,
" my family, whom I love, second to God I love, the future, and I
" prayed for God's love, His wealth, my family not to suffer,
" and I tortured and chained tons, tons, and wrought tons, in, under,
" ships, into the holds, and God's love is this copious ledger,
" God's love is gratuitous, to temper, in me, my children's features,
" porcelain flesh, in a temperless world fearless of God, and
" loveless, unlike God's love of piety, unlike my piety's unlikeness
" and God's distance, I struggle myself, for His love, my sin,
" far from here, I pray for God's love at my hearth pon His science,
" pon His mercy pon the sails pon His ocean; pon His smithy,
" geologies of His silence pon my embarrassment learning to forge,
" the false bottom of God's love, manacles, vicissitudes and
" flesh, whether to cram (1) more, and weather slaving's choiceless
" cost redeemed by untold cost to not bless God's coast, not
" shone His love, His earthly rewards pon His pious lot pon the sea.
" I heard an abolitonist lived in one of my sties, vainglorious,
" he beat his children for common playing and failing at recitations
" of Scripture, he knew men of all portions, a flaunt, he beat
" his wife, too, for her humiliation at his pride in his impoverishing
" Godlessness, and love for his neighbors, though he fucked
" all their wives, and he hardly slept one night in his own sty's bed.
" I have my family read the Holy Bible pon the hearth warm
" stour my cockles in my own juices, God's love, and His logisitics,
" nothing I would not do for my family, the mercantile heart

" of my community, God's love to bear my worth, a name of force,
" bound to God's love, bountiful, beautiful, pon our Atlantic …"

" One of the greatest of the island's sugar plantations has been
  converted into a rambling
" And varied resort. Slave quarters have been remodeled as pastel-
  tinted cottages.
" The sugar mill is a shop. And the former cane fields are a golf
  course, whose fairways
" Sweep down to dazzling water. A few years ago, a quiet bay was
  echoing to the
" Stone mason's hammer and the carpenter's saw. Today, unerring
  tastes and far-sighted
" Planning have made of romantic old ruins luxurious lodgings.
  Modern beachfront real
" Estate, tucked away behind sea grapes and palm groves. With the
  beach and water last
" In a door-yard. Well, those were the changes I saw, more delightful
  dwellings, offering
" A life of indulgent ease. Yet, for all these innovations, the island's
  captivating
" Spell has not been altered. Radiant sunshine. The unmarred
  splendor of beach and sea."

IV. Sea Come Track

Cheek to cheek, limbos dispel, in
    A mill's red shadow. Wet stocks,
        O'er cold harbor, war's breath, are shallow,
            Fucked decisions by livid pratfalls
                Fulminous, steeled in advances, falls, persons
Corpse-usurpations rip from, oars in
    Near to the stairs of mourning,
        Cow eyes, stone vastnesses saints tallow
            With, their following, lo, a rainbow scud
    Time weakens.
Surveillances hanged constellations
    No metaphors budge. O'er
        The dead the salvagers remonstrate:
            I get who I want: relic ache
                Floating webbed vanes unbetrothed
Of you. Inviolate. Kinvein. Ilkskein.
    O, sea come track of bloodplain's use. To
        Bow stroke gestures (s)hackles. To
            Stroke bow gestures; (s)hackles; coxcomb waves
        Preen crow's row's indulgence's profanation.
Staves, in such cries I know you, O, love.
    A breaker extenuates no rows
        Plotted roses inscaped against instressed
        Sound, to evidence, things not heard,
            None anchor to. O, past your eyes waves
Salt wind caress plays burden loss's pain.
    Bound, timing is faith unbewound, sinken, risen, sinken,
        To casus belli, the ground holdless,
            This distance distance sheaths unsheaths,
        To reckon, waves pitiless, is war-footing.
War-footing in the boileries dance granulates.
    The love plot to die, sings the love plot to kill.
        The love plot to kill, sings the love plot to die. Breath's earth.

In Swatchel-Cove

The most opaque
Confers of sufferation.
Guignol, Punch,
Judy, Janey, Jeanne,

Coital tempers are
Whipsawed,
Broke the fever in
Horn-mutes,
Stifled with accessed
Air, settled by

Mouth, saprophytic
Harbinger,
Hucks far what a doll
Cottons to, wagers on,
Pines for,
Unstoppled.

History, cued music at
Pitch put
To screws,
Notched in bedpans,

Nailed on bedposts.
Bastard, *bitte*,
You most know
I command you.
Unlikeness, tongue, say
With a tongue of teeth,

Say twice twice.
I am host, too,
To history. Voices are
Most host to me.

The Etymology of Union

Life is slime—by anfractuous gates—wardens balkanize
The unparolable ground downward—and is—tried alone—
To no one power rooms anesthetize—and life is—sacred—

Numbed hand—none outermore than—to Cotard approx.
INRI contorted—the outermost part tried alone—Culprit—
How will you be tried is no question—the saffron suffix—

The towns and prisons incarnate and vigil—on hawthorn
Owl looked out on light towers—swallows on onlookers—
Destroyed blood—ored life immobilizes on cleanth dusk—

Night—leaves of life to come—again burning—whispers
Extirpated—who are unredeemed—and are not unnamed—
Rose none thrust on hornéd see—thrusting—none seated—

Cowper sat and you fell—prone stour—to the head of the
Corner—ashen—faced—accompaniment—after martellos—
Calvinizing is touch violated and weathered—it is prison—

After martellos—no one without division ranks—to turn
Again—noting among rods and holes and bars one view—
And the stairs grind and blush downward concentration—

Nothing not so green fawning—once over can bear again
Contraptions and shitted tents—condensations turn again—
Culture inside still and humid—flowered the amorous lot—

I am the foundation and the death—for the wages of time
Is concentration and a thousand reservations—I can hold—
I am created to die in one view—all loves are corruptible –

Before us and before us—hot to black start Andersonville
National Prisoner of War Museum—heretofore—
None—not the guest book nor tree-line reclined in repose—

Presently to visit to search a literal sharelight with its lost
Who could liken to escape—as imaginary as true—IMHO—
Life is phobogenic—down the street and across the ocean—

Cruel and decorous the cool morning and wastrel grooms
Over pastels slabs—the colors suborned to perjuring light—
Marbling visitors and prisoners—say any one born to you—

You survived—Say the placards—the exhibits and glyphs
To wide whiteness—in the style editors ploy this drywall—
Unflinching—with with—prejudice witness—Napoleon's—

Dartmoor draughtsmanned—the other globe—uninverted
Plantation eye—irises of naught—insides to many amidst—
Palisades—the currents of exception torched—arced eyes—

Upward to see—who is to say—the viscera of my retort
In-the-body—is—up-for-grabs—my bowels lose control—
Near—before—first panel-distance runs me out to wash—

Rooms—outside death tent thought to be placed in place
Hard to muster—mustered out—musters to enter—I must—
Change shirts—for another before—I re-enter—hollowed—

Ground—tracks—measures—tapes no one writing in the
Macon State Prison—guest book—five point six—miles—
Apart—both powers rooms—collapses roars—a tarrying—

Flickering Mechanicsville

A hang fire, a panicwreath,
A latex siren.
What probes. Everywhere
Is stable vices in the wind,
Linotypes
Of horse logic, look, citrine
Deserters
Reap a wide gap from
The stick-to-itiveness
Of pickets
Of soldiers.
Hole-ups, hold-outs,
You vomit,
I dry-heave.
Cumberland eels branch off duende,
Synchronized with new shore-leaves. Your
Vocative is
Misericord,
Feels with its point, under thwart, whets
The double-
Bind plied at runnel end.
Plinth habits of rostrum.   Circa. Era.
Mass depiction
In weather of low visibility, self-portraiture
Blows fireward more than the
Sovereign flower dogs does. Blood rose ruse.
You interrogate
Necropolitans with a gavage of air.
Who breathes follows knots wince.
Turnkeys in a Q&A
Filmed turkey shoot.

The red-lined
Tantivies embed, brook a grammar,
Aweigh ahead.
Between your eyes, and, elsewhere,
Love, outlasts
Maydays, no-drills. Allies, made by.

Rappahannock Succor

Books read like a loser, analysize
The generals' lives, my life
Substitutes a soldier of peroration.
          Nakedness pans moisture, sheets pan
          Nib web, my just endowment a boon
          To my solitude wounds your solitude.
You hear a sanctuary volunteer when
You hear vacancy sign lightning dim
You hear a blue skullcap lighten skin.
Your dry spills ensconce Verona, Virginia.
          Rocks green, sanctions brown
          Out, on Stone Mountain hobnail
          Out, jut of wanton trajectories
          Footfall, minds surveil a revisionist
          Passage, whose walls, ends at permission,
          Ladders brim vigneron lips, dry gloss fruit glass.
          Losses scrape, the skins make
          Heat. The strangers wipe your sweat.

               'The Windfucker'

Looks read at consent, deracinate
The stranger key, my key
Steps miles, enforces a free fancy.
          Was this a massacre, and I knew that
          Lambkin Strether called me, Live all
          You can, and hanged up phones with
His glovéd hand. The ships sail for a
Clement one. I only ever calm down
In a hotel room, located, or anon. On
          Pergola walls breathed, ragged, fleeces of
          Creatureliness, windy knives
          Chime a porn tune, la vita nuda
          Spotless lawn of storms, bios

In cape castles Norway honed qua
Double-bookkeeping. I'm quarter quisling.
Explicitness runneth off, somebody killed crossing.
The ships sail for a clement one.
The oblige creates a brittle attention.

Fort Pillow Motor Inn

Mazes prise hearts from lives for good
Induction, to stress that good
Pulses leak investors a killing for good
Reduction, to stress that good.

If gangs are dauphins before a righting.
Judas hole of suicide righting.
If gangs fuck guard gangs is it righting.
Judas hole of suicide righting.

Appomattox Agape

Stillness, deadly

Familiar, apropos bows.
New motion is

Stillness at. That

Lovers follow hollowly
Tip to tail, feather

To head, blocked out by

Time, blocked
Out by love. Stillness

Everywhere, but here.

One substance.
You die, before you move

Stillness out of your mind.

What you wish grips
You. Love, everywhere love,

But here, love stillness.

Love, motion, here.
You fail everywhere but here.
A true function of your mind.

Acquiescence (story deprives)
Off-roads with a fish

Bow and a fish arrow.

You fish a quiet piece of time
A quiet peace of love—Dust

On the road sets in,

Fished love and fished time,
Stillness rips open

Stories into storms.

Once, love, with time, coming
Here, were fish here,
Stillness everywhere else.

The arrow hides in the air.

The Boston Evening Traveller

I. A Detail among the Whore Colloquy in Ann Street's "Black Sea"

The cursed portion, la part maudite
Shone harm's welfare, sun dross through
Infection's grille of cloud.
Proof the rack, the eye's gutter and other love surgeries,
Antiseptic rainbow plunges in a bit of muslin,
Mutton in a cape, the hypodermic state draws blood up,
Sterilized under the color of law.
Porcelain organ of the soul, vitrified by shelling
From sconce and cell, to surfeit the skin.
Blood in dumb-show drawn warfare pools on the surfaces.
Lighting of the lamps, serialized upon the stoned-out eyes.
Spermaceti lit rooms swam with upon the stoned-out eyes.

The whores (you do not know) vuln to feed
The beating heart to Jonahs, deserters
To remembrance, commit to passages
To inflict passages the gorge to lie on waits
The ditch that buries distinction waits
To reify along a corpse-scarp branches in casualties
That furcate suspirations from disemboweled steam
To spew the flesh of breath recording
The air, sphered by putrefaction, deem the qualia in
The shithouse is rank with police who feed the meat
Out of the eater to sate the klaxon hoofbeat;
Dull Gret will, with her beacon, stare, come, sign fire.

II. A Detail amid Washington Goode's Death in Leverett Street Jail

And then forced to spew tarred rope,
Spurt forth plug tobacco, pried from his throat, and
Wardens bound the sailor to revival,
Shroud, in white material, his crown scraunched
Heavy with battening, against resurrection,
Violated back to flesh, tied to chair to be hanged,
Police's this anti-anástasi.
Then sat no time's passage on ekkremannumic hell,
Thus the world went out when the words erred o'er.
Sun to altar of the human, breeding,
Came then no one unpelted by the ocean,
No portals given exit, trental prism,
Covered with lights, without sanctuaries,
With racial legal fictions, obvolute
Fields nous pitched, ochred to alibi the chalk's lynching cloud,
Palimpsest night glassed over thrutched men here.
The ocean barking through swamps, the blows and the landed,
Use's theodicy of violence.
Here still they enamour, mine lover and mine lover,
And drawing word from mine hip
I taxed beds with sacrifice;
Pinned high tarred sheets upon each, the love-plot,
First nova of sign to come,
Then the skies the sheets lie on stone in the closer,
A bellum intestinum riven on breakers,
The doubting sand flashes, lacrymatory tides shear,
Gulls dive, a fulmine, where silence castigates.
Dusk, who blushed like it, who led it, in cuffs;
Souls out of Springfields, burr air blurs negation
Of ecologies and the freed enslaved,
Souls defiled summary litanied human sacrifice,
No one a souvenir children with knives tore for,
Battle spoil, bearing no-thing away,
These many crowds about me; with shouting,
Pallor me, patriotic gore against the sky;

Graven on the flesh, slain on fetish,
Cracks the lark till the last glume dews its final fun,
To glory fire's property reflecting porcelain;
Causeless, unknotless thrum,
I put the yellow needle to my deaf ear drum
Till I could hear what sound.
But first Elmina, antiheaven Elmina,
Unsoiled cape, sea gates blush sorest the earth,
Limbs that no one left under mercy's trees,
Unwept, unforsaken in antimemoria,
Pitiless heart.   And I cried in poisoned speech:
"Elmina, thou art how to this dark coast come.
"Stand without, and let nobody come in,"
                    And in the measure mysteriously gone:
"Ill-starred and sponge-thrusted wine.   I slept in hell's mutiny.
"Wearing hard on the strong sea unscrupuled,
"No one fell out as naught might,
"Oughtened the medusan nut, Coriolan americanus.
"But thou, homo sacer, no one curse forget no one, uncivil, unwarred:
"Strike up mine tune, be music by skirmish, and ran through:
"*None of them knew the color of the sky.*
"And drown my oar out, that I pumped for bellows."

And lost causes come, as I puked from, and then anti-Reconstruction,
Holding Hobbes' staff of terror and insertion:
"Another nadir? what? faith of ill belief,
"Violating the dispossessed and this unfallen closer?
"Stand for to the cut, bear no one no bloodless word
"For to lie on."
                    And I pitched forward,
And no one not weak in gratuitous fantasia said then, "Orpheus
"Coming through slaughter, under the vocative blur of the stars,
"Lose not the sound."   And then the aurora carnated.
Lay on, Orpheus. I mean, that is Washington Goode, (Sam Hose) (   )
In nec inops dicendi canticum, 1849, (1899) (   ) out of *The Red Record.*
And no departure no outer peace a handshake meets
And unto nothing.

Sanctus sonus non sine sonus,
In a poet's half-deaf corroded phrase, mustered into liquid
siftings' Antietam, *Coriolanus vocatus est, quod violare usque
ad sepulcrum constituit infernum,* notches in the bedpost
burn, thine voices with dark intercession,
bearing the black boughs of wet petals. Fuck it:

II

The Rings of Saturn

On the media
Miens aspect a fair-grounds
The glad crowd rolls
What grows with its own
Image boasts and prowls
Outside. Families
With incisors for heads
Satisfy and beam
Image, a way of life, ruptures
The ground apples and shares
After-life. Inside
Draft wheels scrape walls
And, off-balance, scrawl: —
Property is Father of the Man.
Countenance:
Kodaks of a hundred of
Numberless of
A night and broken
Narrativities evidentiary eyes
Find the angle.
The observation wheel
Keens up, a riser in
Nighttime, purloins
Fear and loneliness, even
Omitted, surplus, inadmissed.
Sent de trop made
A place for self aside self
Forced on. Self-hate, self-murder,
Self-rape. Eyes
Avert what rushes forms
Pangs obverse fate.
Oblivion, oblivious, opaque.
To whom the eyes
Owe the sight. My eyes in
Photographs look like the
Left eye of Joseph Merrick.

Poison Oak Candle for Southern Agrarians

I

Fuck personality, thought

> The genial genius.
> The nail inspector, after a
> Tour of the planks,

> > Cried, O sylvan memento

> O featureless death
> The rows in the stave hold
> *The rose in the steel dust*

Internal and internal rhythm do nothing

> > Unforbidden, without—Elaborate—
> > Exploit—The crowd to dowse the source—
> > Habiliments of skin widen circles—

> > Ripples—Thrashes—Whirlpools—Ram-rods!

II

The ash-larder you holed up

    In tarnished, before
    The chain-oil industry-swell.
    The ransom house

        Spins spider holes, races air

    In a gossamer globe.
    Property if cuneiform skirls
    The airfield of a pipeline,

Just a terror of steam visible in the cold air.

        The guard and the gardener, visaged
        In heraldic masks, gaff cannon
        Fodder up. The semantics, pennants,

    Lick it. The mass grave recoils.

III

Meditation feebly waits for

    Desolated lambs are
    Bred in an underpass to the
    Meat plant, country

        For non-fiction. What you

    Do know, what you
    Can't know, heady in dutch,
    Evangelized the seamless

Extradition kidnap coast. Don't look now,

        Where dusty mallets will swing next.
        Landed arils ruck open moral
        Landscape. Besieged literacy a quota

    Widens to undergird casualties.

IV

Actors sound awful at acting.

> I am risk-averse. I am
> Pleasure. I have not thought.
> I'm fucked. On a wave

> > Even the palliator is smitten,

> Bell-churn of self-rung
> Script. The gall flavor spalls,
> *Heimweh* on the fritz, thus,

Thrownness tallows the toy ball I cannot

> > Retrieve, affixed to freeze-frame, its
> > Dead, its quotational soldier,
> > Fretted down its meal car and gulled a

> Place-setting. I cannot stand it.

V

Navigate,

Lowered,

Against death, Belief.

Mud-flagged, any

March

Fêted 'll thick.

VI

In love, oblique house, quartered

>   With a voyeur, heart
>   In the mouth digs out a wretch
>   All, red white of fear,

>   Tabula rasa flight toward

>   Star fens. Unmoored
>   Kierkegaard bailiff constellation.
>   Of stars, size is eaves-

Taken size; of stars, siege is eaves-taken.

>   Wound, tongue, lubricant, neighbor.
>   Windows glow, shame undisclosed, honor.
>   Wound, tongue, lubricant, neighbor.

>   Windows glow, shame undisclosed, honor.

VII

Your grave tenderness flits a

    Red match, its genius
    Loves no flue goes up for
    You. If only belletrist

        Lit, why can the buttercup's

    Murderer see out ere,
    Ambivalent, splendid, points
    South neglects forms

Mixed chastity, alloy only a portion virgin,

        The spiritual crank, lament haft both
        Unturned and nothing on crane.
        Rock-drill by dint of reconstructions

    Social ploy—My love, you

VIII

You get misspoken, subject

    Positions, or Subject
    Gets positioned, as fortress
    Aerial views promise,

        Your insides fill rocket hills,

    With gasconade I am
    Not a man, I am Coriolanite!
    Lionized. I learn to state.

Marbled. Boughs drip watchful and rumors

    Over infantry bald with baseness. Rage
    Exerts inwardly, perspires stings, its cod-heat
    Basks inwardly, visages suns, freights a

Saturnine beam. Weary. Sweat, glove gives.

IX

Mirror visible, steam read:

Unwon: strop shorn
The gentry culture of air, a
Warlock, en brosse:

Violence scorns itself most:

Do not think you do
Not believe what is obverse
To your low actions,

Peaceful though be, seem,

Obsequy as certain to pass through
Harm, harmlessly, fingers through a twenty-
Twenty vision of a twenty-year-old

Girl, hair, eyes do not err her spare youth,

X

Prosecute,

Vexed,

Against death, Belief,

Yawn, chasm, any

Wake

Debted 'll pitch.

XI

Death quartered the streets,

Tar late rain beads
In steam-lock pipe seals
2nd skin, isinglass,

      Behind whatever it quarters.

Fort! Da! Now the
Occupied town throws
Their civilians and

      Now their bay troops retrieve

The ball they sally they vocal
Ridges peace in the cut shone violetly
On sacral roads they engineer

Pavers tar enmity, gleaners v. yeomen.

XII

In troughs of WD40 bayonets squidded bloody soils.

Picaresque vista, instagrafts, horizons spike
In a martial present, a martial past, a future
Martial ontology, greensward in script on a

Spine of any ward—'Death By Water' babbles, in the
Dock, intrudes on Pip in the dusk of the mast, even to
Lose one's mind places a presence: white indifference.

Testify on the rack, as nullification
Starts the fit, shits and movements
Fall away. Parties and sorties vault

Tribunal moon ice brightens, petals of axes.
Mutinize space that gives, clots, and shapes,
Raum, shirt, boat, drownt *Phoenician Sailor.*

XIII

Tighten your idols, wheel, in the rise your death

    Where as a pageant,
    Drift ruined garden,
    Ark of clay pigeons,

Hark your supervention, dancer, but not the dance, rifled trifle.

        Steel, vortices breeze

In Blackmur a moral christmas, Tate a
Palest blackface, lo, rhetorical figures
Who color in whiteness. That diegesis,

    Like blackface, fire-sale oxymoron, a white burden.

Eliot a violet evening coverages green and ball
With everybody, that privity privacies.
Mahagonny falls through a near ocean   (2018–2020)

    'I identify with everybody.'

XIV

Fair shimmer wastes outside health tents

My body slides across a floor
The spider nipples the hearth
Apostasy

Tree or hole hire me and ditch me

Pools
Of martial narcissisi fanned
Wedged in beached mortises

In the dawn, Black, naval,
Under bloody shirt fronds a penal stripe
Looms, goes pear-shaped.

Theodic malison, pepper and pineapple,
Sweats paper, the pool smell of wounds.

XV

Transubstantial,

Survived,

Against death, Belief,

Ultra, vires, any

Nota

Nailed 'll prick.

XVI

A fence hides a light you

Think sacrificial.

In spire strike a light you

Think dungeons

Leaps forsook.
On atonement
Apologia burn.

Courage ladders its paucity
With great obsequiousness,
Nothing tropical minted by

A dance a rigid wisdom eyes plea grant
You space in gait theurgy, a magnetism.
A volition drains. Play a bar with a hole.

XVII

     Shame develops allegory alchemy
     To make your heart appear in the darkroom
     Without question a question, tree or soldier.

Between reality and the black swans
Why keep life sprung against
Orders. With trees or soldiers.   A plea of blue alluvions.

     A tree is an ethic in proportion to the visible.
     People think time = war. Your soldier stands
     Still, a consumer of thought, in total portière.

       Nature signs the age under bulls-eye.
       Intimacy aligns margins base to base.
       National autumn loves broken blades.

Red shapes, amid slats of trees and soldiers, diminish.

XVIII

Is your tongue not as tongue as. I find ways I am not human.

What apportions excepts, exeunt,
Bound-less, Love,
Love love had better being about you not be.

Illegitimate, illegible, ineluctable.

The rainbow bangs a storm in, in
A bend uncompromised.
American Romanticism,   Reason, prismed

A rope of smaller ropes, prisons   Sightless field, a limit

When you liken, you incur against.
What if you were all teeth.
Kissed by another bitter revelation.

Nobody is just.   No love is just.

XIX

Subtle argument, the line
Denatured, a sentimental
Street, and sex evergreen.

A fatal flaw.

How many times
Up and what
Sunk your voices.

Bound are services my law
Thy to, goddess
My art, nature, thou.

Paradise whole halves worse off
Without whole halves worse off,
O, deem 'off' visible as bastardy.
After-life a half-deaf eavesdrop on a bastard gathers.

Now gods

Now gods   XX

                     Now gods

Juxtapose,

Dazzled

Against death, Belief,

Perfect, perfect, any

Scales

Mirrored 'll strike.

The Vegetable Lamb's Entry
into Charleston in 1858

La plante a chair et sang, l'animal a raçine
                                    Du Bartas

Area de nostra nunc est tibi facta ruina;
conspicuum uirtus hic tua ponat opus.
                                    Ovid

Onlooker's choice bounds by your procession,
Nothing beyond the standard flows collect
Not forfeit to vastation, not rain, bearings wet,
Over eccentric bowls bled white incession.

Rows attest to vicissitudes, a dueness.
O, harvest such cast intrinsic and just.

Sirens the lamb to the bush
Wet graft's weal
Tar set, no lanolin for song,
Speech I sport it,
Soil loss roots amalgamate.

Darkness, the paint of time,
Reads to the master,
Flowers. Tracing nothing even yet
All points bulletin musicking
Transfers wool's worth rows office.

Otium's tune...my factory's central crucible
Bears the retinue's organs, huller and gin,
To corner acedia's halo-load, head leaden in
Bloodless illumination, fainthearted, utile.

Rose's goad: villa's blood at the ready.
Ovid's cuple fleshes coigns by the sea.

Votives to the dust, anthropic fury flurries.
Save your roses. Save your air.
Crowds confess breezes alighted on what
Is the oil to come, Love. Love,
Bitter warmth, you cost your name I do it.

I am like Matthew, I count when, when

When did not. Outside, the bales, roads
Shone, sky bolling shone to no one
Nothing, without the mine-white covet.
I tail realization, I try to spell assail.
Your rolling breaches white loam ashes
Conceal, after day without sea level,
Without nudities, what seals. Darken
Shores shone one, a sail, a seal, a sale.

The importation of cotton into Liverpool and London in 1886 was as follows:—

	lbs.
American	1,317,562,480
Brazilian	33,832,400
Egyptian	173,340,000
West India, etc.	9,529,910
Surat	148,306,700
Madras	26,729,200
Bengal and Rangoon	32,324,600
Total	1,741,625,290

The Etymology of Union

Buy Orchestrions!
I own one so no song cognates
Race rings voices
Without! continental prosthetic

I have no musical face
Ecology does not preface;
I have no musical face
Ecology does not surface;

Enlightenment loves,
The subject, is peace,
In the capital, reason,
It rains, in name only,

Forward: a quartz sound file:
Quartet home concert: filial
A photo obtrudes: afterglow:
Backs of faces face lynching.

Freely effaced with names ˙
Invented souvenirs
Modern what ends of mind
In the palms callus

The wounder
The disfigurer,
The wounder
The dishesion.

Wave of brims on law fire.
White album a bleb
Slows an object on a black
Stylus spindle plinth.

Re-Enactment

Brecht kept no remorse in
Time he hashed
Fit to remorse us.
We kept us upstream blood
On rinsed hands.

Front line nailed the wall,
Flank, ripple, fall,
Battery sang try to not hit
Yourself too hard,
War drags life, its usufruct,
In the balloon, we
Fucked, gear in the basket.

Show me the glad couples who
I can show you a few
Gyre torture themselves
Over their heads. You do this thing
Your brain tells you to do.
If you are not in jail by
Day's end, you cheated, you knew.
Horizontal collaboration:
You learn to cheat
Backslides into death. No one gets less than
One slot.

Your ears are hot mala fides
About the hermit of history,
Invisibly dimmed the H of H.

Scaffolds crowd into a crowd of aegis.
Historical etymology: Horns: Spectral

Projection of what is human,
Too late aloft, what is human, plus.
Love hates so many, I'll not
Imply its presences, upon regimes
Regiment whomever her overlord.

The Gods of Repositories

We ask who is
Missing several ways.
Did hair-shirts
Interdict hair,
Did scruples screw
In a face.
The blood parts snared
Pedestals

Voice over. Stone walls
Wash wish white
Music for Black people.
Rhetorical figure
Knaves are, nails unlike

       With life.
       Parts
       Sun,
       Starves tasted
       Piss outlived
       Hell now and again,

       Billfolds lowed
       In grass woke to a shirt
       Mid-babble
       With night feelers.
       Throw good
       Soldiers after bad
       Wake to the

Night surgeon, etc.
Throw maggots,
Lay hearts. Skin on
Skin parts.
Doctrines on billfolds.
Means on battlefields.

Not My Horses

Not actions not quite words
But under such dates
Belie the black flags to rink
Plazas in ice and till
Ring-roads to pieces, until
Time is no longer pat
Velvet jacketed with blood
Shed by basilisks nor
Chained up on colonnades,
Until I see what you see
The pennant no one waves.

Whit Women

Whit women
Prink garnets. Espy a jaw
Suck beaujolais.
Gender and
Other nightmares
Inside war deem pretense.
Women wore
Shiloh raiments at a bloody
Angle to feel
On the bloody angle.
Women with
Her toy spleen and chemical grief
Fucked to mourn with public guts.

Epoxy eyes
Net above carbuncle gaits.
Sentimentality
Rides a proxy heart.
Rain down the face, dirty steps.
Approximant
Courthouse of
Feelings.
The rüb the road
Deputized for a sanguinary desire.
Soft brief
For the defense
Kitted out in public mourning.

This, a chance I am
Laced as a castle,
Ugliness, is what I earn.
Entrances light
Whales of buildings,
Bend sinister.
The end of love is intimacy.

I do not need you.
You love me.
You want to kill me,
More than life,
I want your expression.
Pries from thy resonance me up.

Excoriated Station

Emplotment tilts glasses for
Knowledge, titles what you and I are
Convulsed about, importuned
In a booth.
Its titian-on-black homilies
Smear the face, unction, and waits
Dress in a bred
State, for the face au fait
With. Wet felt of time sum darns over new
    Uniform, homily. Student-soldiers
    Open their mouths
    Wide perch on, before song, teeth
    Seen, at corners of lips, after song
    Seen at the front.
    Nether crying jags lure

Depiction. L'ANSE is ripe with smoke
Brassieres allure, edge, their
Pastel apparitions
Whose durable cells charge its parlor
Analcime lit, with a Sobraine gold-tip
Passed in a circle
The birth-mark, a certain lip plushes forth embars
Open at the covet.
    Phrases in sulfur and cloth quotes of color, in
    The eyes of, THE COVE. Visages eyes
    Shun freeze out skin, plumb solemn. In
    Parsimony glass, eggs brine Fabergé, vermilion.

        Names written in reverse blood on glass,
        Bad-faith tan, Wide Awake or kill squad.
        The dancers make looks a pommel horse.
        The gag's a promiscuous reflex of orders.

Novitiates wedged and did not defend,
The pitilessness of pity, Hill's fixed against,
A love-wail, alighted owls flushed out,
Lead in crossfire lattice, deadlocked quarry.
The gaudy honor point, be true enemy.
Scrupulosity lulled backslid and Judgement.

III

Nail Sickness: Boston Common

Antagonized by knowledge base, I mean bad faith

Against thought, a thought slags, the fireclay faith

A fire imbricates offscum ember flown, flue toxin

Ablution, each brick, a threshold, the devils tocsin.

Altaforte

CIVIL FRUIT: *En* Thomas Jefferson.
Ezra Pound raked that life over Heaven with what he
tried to make Paradise.
Ecco lassù il castello!
Spare me!

Sift his laurel foulings to the coils.

The picture is in his plantation, Monticello. "Jemmy" is
his collaborator, Madison. "Water American," the anonym of Franklin
(Lion Erect).

I

Blast today, this underwent days perish from, fidelity
To treed sun. Monticello mori blots out terroir
Withal build its peculation eclipses Jemmy streamed.
Water American, Lion Erect, earwig the media
Who slut his effigies in terrorface, bedstraws labored
In austere hand, scribbled shipping containese supine.

II

Virginian luxuries, slide I the currency supine,
Over groping furor, such cup-and-ball fidelity,
And the rights of man sucked mutable, property labored,
And the nightingales unsex me, their stour across terroir,
And Hyperion wanes crops tax boats haul back to media,
And the stiffened wake cloth and corn long for, a grail wound
    streamed!

III

Rank, tested the baseless consolations, dishonour, streamed
I without figure. Turncheek, tastes each razor shell's supine
Blood that creams blandish. Eau du postures, my shaved media,

My life of Christ, I shall not want miracles, in Heaven's fidelity.
Blow, candled warden, hide love's fame, Psyche's heart-eaten terroir
His rings and waxes sealed, the snuffed out rapes, the smoke labored.

IV

When light is your auction block...natural manure labored
Wings...and butchery gives air morning portals octaves streamed...
Blueprint gardens lot and pile, orchestrations grade supine...
Then light, revoice me my disfluencies of you, my quartet words terroir
Sheds destroyed, loved to pieces, cut snake, ah, fidelity!
Curse the heart's walling fruit, come intertissued media!

V

Up no one, shyly Jefferson, green stars fuss their media.
Contrive, architect, marble's liquid plantation's labored
Plasticity. Pulvers to pounce secure fidelity,
Not words. Security wealth tours, its humans streamed
In post-gore gift shops their pre-gore softcovers supine
In which for a long time is called waiting on the terroir.

VI

Jemmy, Jemmy, let's curettage firmament from terroir!
Love, my love is coloring terror, ah spring, fust media
Tours, form colleges of men to rot out riot reason supine
With killed women, to explain the windows belabored
Nat'l razor reflections. Biopower Lion Erect streamed
Fugal state notes, 'Let's star Sally Hemings in a Fidelity

VII

Ad, insured against her will: first verse, means, last verse labored
Ends, by the sea the incommutable undergoing streamed
A part from a whole star shipped supine forget you forget fidelity.'

Bloody-Minded

No perfect liberator come
In creatureliness
Raps vitrics; spurns; aggrieves.
Is your ethic bad timing.
Is life with you fatal, non-
Plus, a flaw on love on behalf of.

Web or fly, swither not
Who I love, but do
I web, do I fly, or you return.
Place shit with words
Locale backmasks
Surfaces curl, key-brief, eels.

Schmitt at land and sea
Sleeves, interpolate
Reciprocity, reportless context
Bisects the world its
Puce keen. Yes? Yes. No
Question, arachnid supremacy.

Anabasis

Counting is the epistemology of war.
James Dawes

In a sleepless number, the Ego conceives
In the still of the night. In the grain house each degradation time milks
    from its copper mouth
Begins to drip with a clarity caught that begins to look uncertain
    caught next to eventual next,
In clear glass brands, on the rack,
In the shade of that same grain's rainbow. Outside this stalled parable,
    National Guard
Motors start and run our voices together. I mean what I have done to
    you begins to list
In me and once more
I do not hear you, I enlist you—to extract exactness even fumes
    withstand,
Each concession to that self, I allow to breathe, what fortune's rude
    nimbus already wreathes.

That choice in fortune was daft about me.
Shit-stirrer to beach-comber, operatives flare, by dint of windfall, a
    symmetry on fire suffers.
Metallurgy extols the air to dress everyone's looks in their war dead,
    known by their swoons.
Love a shiver, shivers like a coda.
Georgia has Mars, Uncle Billy a cow: war sublimation chastens; a
    bigoted sufficiency;
Peroration gives shape their bailiwick; dysentery hearts swell a bubble
    on a sea of shit.
The eye has a nation,
Hit upon viewfinder: little measure, little ease. Framers precinct
    wingspan,
Swanned uniforms: another country on the installment plan; another
    country a golden means.

You move proof, I wait for parapet's flash.

No health, no wisdom, no love, evening ought weary and treasure, old
enthusiasms fucked in

Apostrophe. By jove to sustain, on a caves' fantasy, a starry starry night
dispossesses vacancy.

Territory, comrades at extenuated.

Gathers buttress your forehead a fort of doubt; in the new terror, it's:
heed one's friend

Illegally; somewhat deaf to fate, honorific, naked with title; fish tastes
how it's packed.

The dyer has a glove

Difference in prescience, empty bath, and marronage, in fruit from
blood.

Ease the gore out of the birth of Josephine, a pigment instructs a wave,
it gulls into open boat.

The spits of waste spoked oblution wheeled
March en plein war, wet fire, lathe animals.
Sewages annotated with sumptuary instress.
Sherman segregated soul, use, and property,
No parts touched at Savannah colloquy and
Yawed one, that roved, amid many gehenna.

Yankee Among the Swallows

Rapesick Ulysses reads his leaves
Cupping his shames on sides to chrism,
The rye café in his boning-white
Interpreting cause to his schism.

The cilices of the mourny sun
Feign servile and free state hotels,
Jubilee and the acres till death
And Ulysses conveys the sea isles.

Bitter zeal and a powder flask
Are aneled; and fleered shrive for song;
The singer in her chaste mask
Swots Ulysses through her Comus

Knots and echoes gibe banquot hall
Overtures, les contretemps
Cozed subdural odes gnaw and gall
Bianca to show more tonsil;

Hygienic prolegomenon
Pumps her heart with humanism;
The dumbwaiter peels patinas,
Erogens, eugenics, and euphemisms;

The auditory voices, bone-in, run
Through, to the life, speak, recite;
Bradstreet *née* Beatrice
Chants 'The Lady,' shrieks *Vol de Nuit.*

Bianca and the lady, miasma
Wet, decamp tweezed, moony narrows
Recta ratio quiver lice at first
Bar of day bayonets shift a pit harrows.

Seawall: Perjury

Is your soul
One hundred per cent wet.

What is consentless

Sands in on fortress

Scours down to fort

Names.

Behind vomit from

Names behind

Pincers rock slimes.

If you ask me to, you puke.
I do, I puke.

Swimmers want food, love.
Red rover

Escutcheon
Between a hole and a key.

To pieces

Real war moves mouths

You-let-me-let-you-sing

Jeanne's injection

Doubt is a future preface.

A harmless song of harm.

The Etymology of Union

Mazes receipt whatever humans name
    Hearts, live urns. One heart
Mopped buttery on the execution floor.
    Cells tally fogs watched out

Of up, ill and crass, nacreous dolphins
    Gang past, without the right
One heart the C.O. airs out a bullet for.
    Can a prisoner fuck a guard.

A compline wound, a catch and release
    Flyleaf, under each sign, the
Sign of incarceration sound is illegible
    With, routines end-men slip

Smiles between the heaves of the heart.
    I do not know how you think
Once person is not possessive—I—not
    Another bromide to serve air

At immurement, angled, view = weight.
    Solitary matters, cento centos
Soledad casque, Livilla, air. The waves
    Ride anabases in seaside bars.

In Heresy Relapse

Before the commune rose the cloister fires
Burned the saint to death at Rouen.
The voices she heard taught her to hie law,
Drag truth across a state to Heaven.
Bark claws itself from birch to the mineral maiden,
Fugitations in stratum, unquarried and unspoken.
Benighted, God set spokes in language,
Stainless cuts her hair bore shibboleths
Dead, bastion to invection's phylactery,
I mistook you, out of the blue
In the bombed alley's chancel.
Wasted sign, a cloud could speak to you.
No still time in war could eclipse gossip.
Voices name their clarity with our waste.
First tent to last nail, the heart tenders fate.

Envoi

Without image, syntax syncretizes weather selves flood, a sound can
   clothes the heart against
   More light,

Terror light moors, set to rights, all-day sun ruminant, darkenedness
   clothes, the close of ease.

Here, a grief cloth muse cannot come spoken, without one auroral one,
   no one just, unspoken.

More hour lay than window between bars in rooms lay faces law bare
   teeth bay song can bite.

Counting downwards days coming is boring a wholly ignored hole's in
   tax heard here, a thud.

Mary Rowlandson Beach House
for Forgiven Narcissists

Do a girl in wistfully
Voices,
Belled from lips
Scaffolds sea perspective.
Exxon dart. Hair
Spangles any mortal

Sprint waters
Vanish in auditory anchors
Waves engulf.
Question pain its music.
Beat blood palm
Above. Arterial guide.

Rain pips the iris, articles
To tears. What are the
Moods for love. Is anyone.
Mag the moon in
Dusk dunes sand
Which grain is forgiveness.

Historic violets steep.
Pill built from fruit pestle,
Hour zero mortared.
You, tenderest astride me,
No energy wastes to
Intimate grace. Hair sword.

Acknowledgments

Many thanks to the editors who first published these poems:

"Anabasis," "The Etymology of Union," "Not My Horses," "The Vegetable Lamb's Entry into Charleston in 1858," "Yankee Among the Swallows," "In Heresy Relapse," and "Envoi" appeared in *The Carolina Quarterly*.

"In Swatchel-Cove" and "The Gods of Repositories" appeared in *Interim*.

"Leviathan" appeared in *KROnline*.

"Flickering Mechanicsville" appeared in *Lana Turner: A Journal of Poetry and Opinion*.

"Rappahannock Succor," "Speculative Fire," and parts of "Poison Oak Candle for Southern Agrarians" appeared in *Prelude*.

"Needle," "Fort Pillow Motor Inn," "Appomattox Agape," "The Rings of Saturn," "The Etymology of Union," "Whit Women," "Excoriated Station," "Nail Sickness: Boston Common," "Bloody-Minded," "The Etymology of Union," and "Re-enactment" appeared in *Second Stutter*.

"Seawall: Perjury" and "Mary Rowlandson Beach House for Forgiven Narcissists" appeared in *West Branch*.

About the Author

MATTHEW MOORE received a BA from Kenyon College and an MFA from the Michener Center for Writers at the University of Texas at Austin. His poetry has appeared in *The Carolina Quarterly, Interim, KROnline, Lana Turner, Prelude, Second Stutter,* and *West Branch.* He is the translator of *Opera Buffa* by Tomaž Šalamun. He has also translated a chapbook, *Padova* by Igo Gruden. His translations have appeared widely in literary journals and magazines, including *Asphalte Magazine, Changes Review, Conjunctions,* and *Gulf Coast.* This is his first collection.